COLDEST PLACES
ON THE PLANET

by Karen Soll

Raintree is an imprint of Capstone Global Library Limited, a company incorporated in England and Wales having its registered office at 264 Banbury Road, Oxford, OX2 7DY – Registered company number: 6695582

www.raintree.co.uk
myorders@raintree.co.uk

Editorial Credits
Karen Soll, editor; Juliette Peters, designer;
Tracy Cummins, media specialist; Tori Abraham, production specialist

ISBN 978 1 4747 1263 7 (hardback)
16 15 14 13
10 9 8 7 6 5 4 3 2 1

ISBN 978 1 4747 1267 5 (paperback)
17 16
10 9 8 7 6 5 4 3 2 1

British Library Cataloguing in Publication Data
A full catalogue record for this book is available from the British Library.

Photo Credits
Corbis: Ann Johansson, 9; Getty Images: Amos Chapple, 15, Daisy Gilardini, 11, Volvox volvox, 7; Ned Rozell: 17; Shutterstock: Anton_Ivanov, Cover Top Right, Avatar_023, 21, gadag, Cover Top Left, Ivsanmas, Map, PavelSvoboda, 5, Sander van der Werf, Cover Bottom, 3, saraporn, 13, 22-23, Volodymyr Goinyk, 19, zebra0209, Design Element, 1
Every effort has been made to contact copyright holders of material reproduced in this book. Any omissions will be rectified in subsequent printings if notice is given to the publisher.

All the internet addresses (URLs) given in this book were valid at the time of going to press. However, due to the dynamic nature of the internet, some addresses may have changed, or sites may have changed or ceased to exist since publication. While the author and publisher regret any inconvenience this may cause readers, no responsibility for any such changes can be accepted by either the author or the publisher.

CONTENTS

COLD PLACES

Some places are very cold.

They may not get sunshine.

Other cold places are

high up. Let's find out

about these cold places.

Life is very cold

on the seafloor.

Sunlight cannot reach it.

The water near the seafloor

is very cold too.

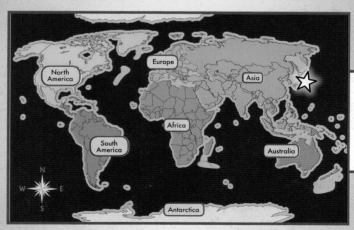

The deep sea is about
1 degree Celsius
(34 degrees Fahrenheit).

Would you sleep on an ice block? A hotel in Sweden is made of ice. People use hides to stay warm when they sleep.

It is -5 degrees Celsius (23 degrees Fahrenheit) in the ICEHOTEL.

9

COLDER PLACES

The North Pole is
at the top of the world!
Sunlight can't reach it
in winter. It can get
very cold.

In winter, temperatures at
the North Pole drop below freezing.
During the summer, it is around
freezing point. This is 0 degrees
Celsius (32 degrees Fahrenheit).

Mount McKinley is
in North America. It is
higher than anywhere
in Europe. Its windy peak
can be very cold.

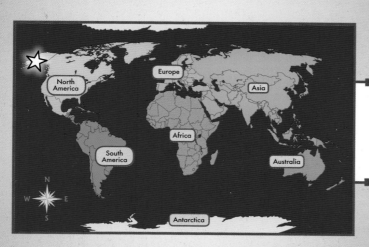

Temperatures at the peak
can feel like -73 degrees Celsius
(-100 degrees Fahrenheit).

COLDEST PLACES

Do you want to live in the coldest city? More than 200,000 people do. This is in Yakutsk, Russia.

The highest temperature in Yakutsk in January is -40 degrees Celsius (-40 degrees Fahrenheit).

Snag is a small town in Canada.

It is the coldest place

outside the Antarctic.

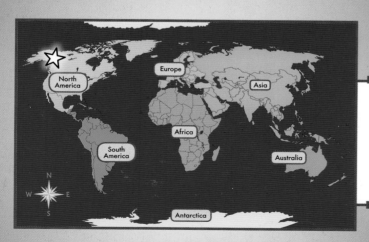

On a February day in 1947,
the temperature in Snag was
-63 degrees Celsius
(-81 degrees Fahrenheit).

The South Pole is
the coldest place
in the world. It never
gets above freezing.

On 21 July 1983, a record low
was set. The temperature was
-89 degrees Celsius
(-128.5 degrees Fahrenheit).

We have learnt about cold places round the world. People can live in these chilly places! Which cold place would you like to visit?

Snowstorms can occur in cold places. This climber was caught in a snowstorm in Alaska.

GLOSSARY

chilly—cold

freezing point—0 degrees Celsius (32 degrees Fahrenheit)

hide—the skin of an animal

peak—the pointed top of a mountain

record—a collection of facts

seafloor—the ground at the bottom of the sea

sunlight—light from the sun

temperature—the measure of how hot or cold something is

READ MORE

Harsh Habitats (Extreme Nature), Anita Ganeri (Heinemann-Raintree, 2013)

Seymour Simon's Extreme Earth Records, Seymour Simon (Chronicle Books, 2012)

Show Me Polar Animals (My First Picture Encyclopedia), Lisa J. Amstutz (Capstone Press, 2013)

WEBSITES

http://climatekids.nasa.gov/polar-temperatures/

Discover which pole is really colder with information from NASA.

http://sevennaturalwonders.org/mount-mckinley/

Learn more about one of the natural wonders of the world.

http://www.worldatlas.com/webimage/countrys/polar/northpole.htm

Read why the North Pole is such a cold, amazing place.

CRITICAL THINKING QUESTIONS

1. Why is it cold on the seafloor? How does the picture help you understand this fact?

2. What might it be like to stay at the ICEHOTEL?

3. The author uses the words "windy" and "very cold" to describe the peak of Mount McKinley. Why might it be described in that way?

INDEX

Year: 2